How to Draw
Aircraft

For Jesse, Jasmine, Justin, Jordan, Melina, and Matthew

Published in the United States of America by The Child's World®
PO Box 326 • Chanhassen, MN 55317-0326
800-599-READ • www.childsworld.com

Acknowledgments
Illustration and Design: Rob Court
Production: The Creative Spark, San Juan Capistrano, CA

Library of Congress Cataloging-in-Publication Data
Court, Rob, 1956–
  How to draw aircraft / by Rob Court.
      p. cm. — (Doodle books)
  ISBN-13: 978-1-59296-803-9 (library bound : alk. paper)
  ISBN-10: 1-59296-803-1 (library bound : alk. paper)
  1. Aircraft in art—Juvenile literature. 2. Drawing—Technique—Juvenile literature. I. Title. II. Series.

NC825.A4C68 2007
743'.8962913334—dc22

2006031557

The Scribbles Institute™

How to Draw

Aircraft

by Rob Court

The
**Child's
World**

seaplane

1

2

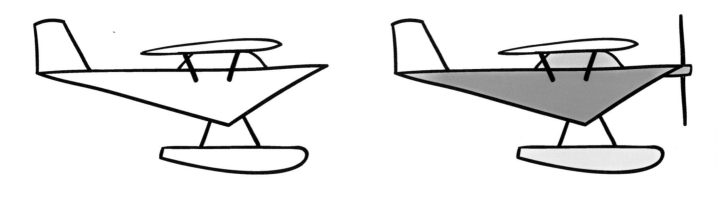

3

4

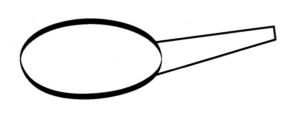

1

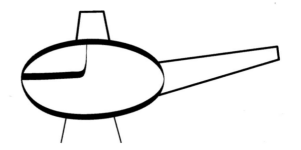

2

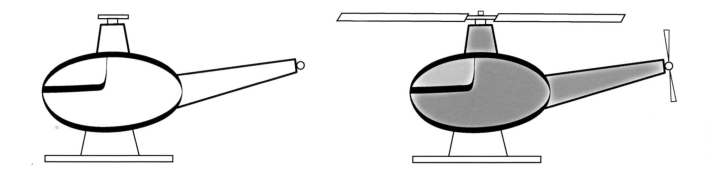

3

4

biplane

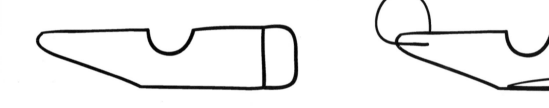

1

2

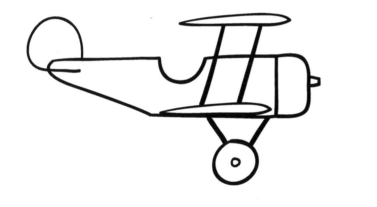

3

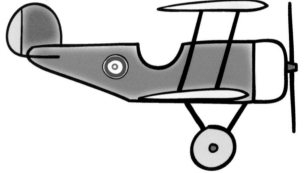

4

blimp

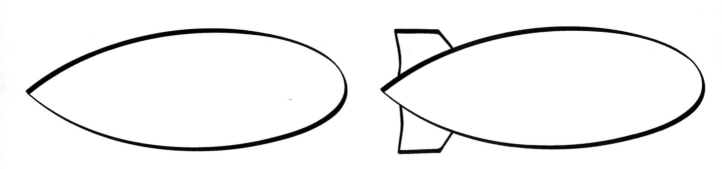

1

2

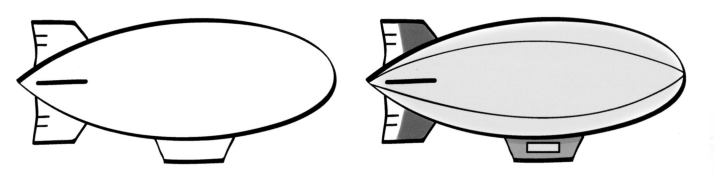

3

4

space shuttle

1

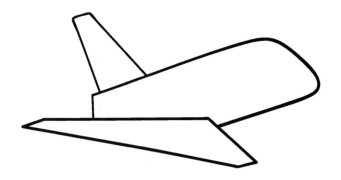

2

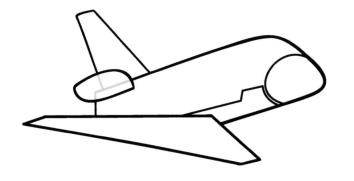

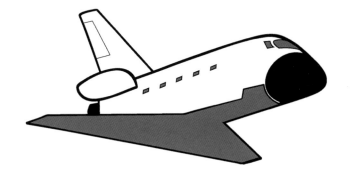

3

4

cargo plane

1

2

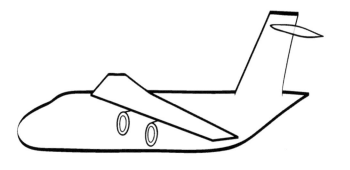

3

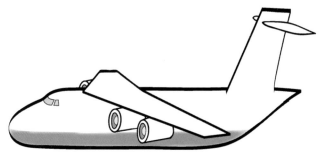

4

glider

1

2

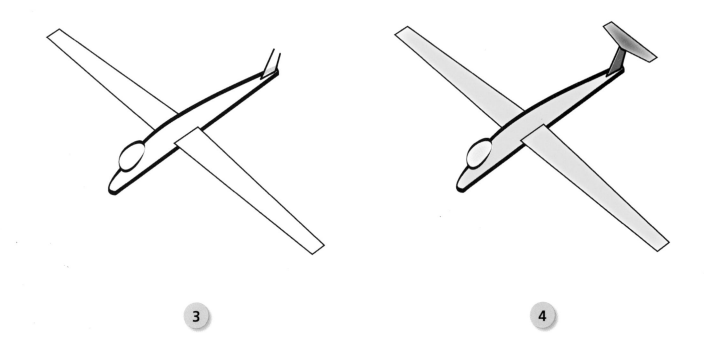

3

4

hot air balloon

1

2

3

4

Harrier jet

1

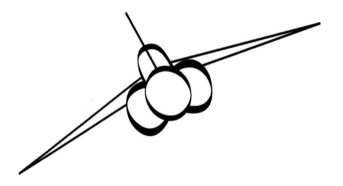

2

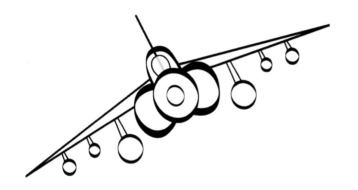

3

4

passenger jet

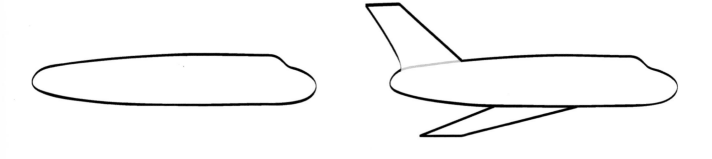

1

2

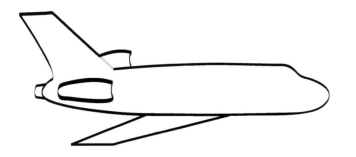

3

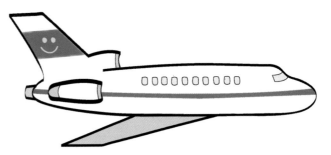

4

commuter plane

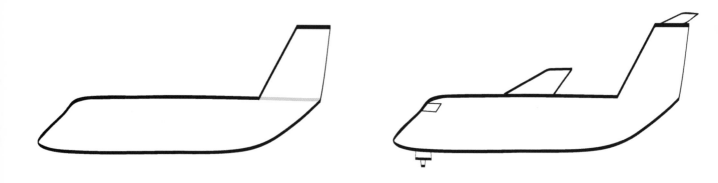

1

2

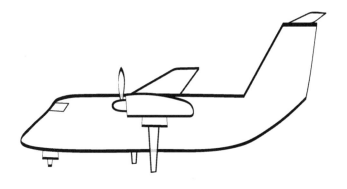

3

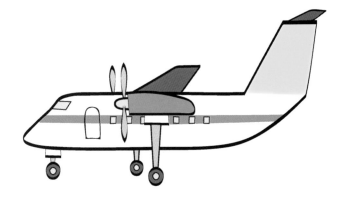

4

1

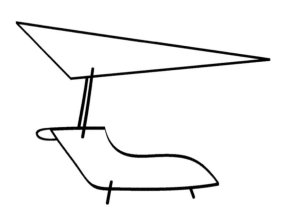

2

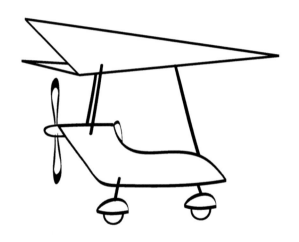

3

4

jet fighter

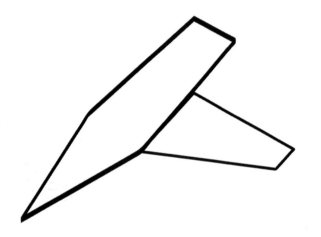

1

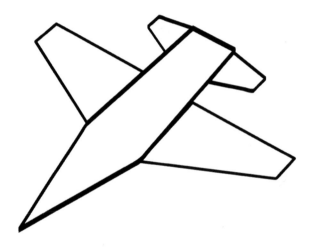

2

3

4

Spirit of St. Louis

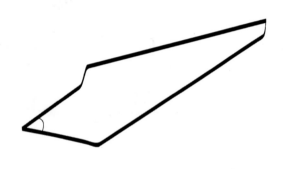

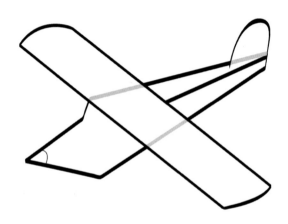

1

2

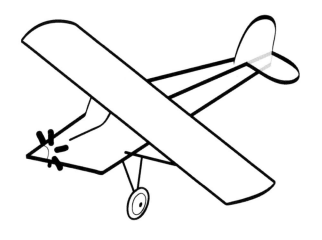

Spirit
of
St. Louis

3

4

lines

horizontal

vertical angled

curved

thick

thin

dotted

squiggly

dashed

point

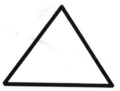
Move a point to make a line.

Connect lines to make a shape.

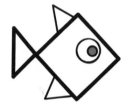
Shapes make all kinds of wonderful things!

loop

Repeating dots, lines, and shapes makes patterns.

About the Author

Rob Court is a graphic artist and illustrator. He started the Scribbles Institute to help students, parents, and teachers learn about drawing and visual art. Please visit www.scribblesinstitute.com